1

Trash Island

A tragicomedy of ecological proportions

by

Neil S. Reddy

For Sue

Published by Dank House Manor Publishing 2018

dankhousemanorpublishing@gmail.com

Trash Island

A tragicomedy of ecological proportions

Written for the stage by Neil S. Reddy

THE CONCIET

Susan is the only child of a religious zealot whose beliefs are at odds with the world around him. His wish to protect his daughter conceals his drive to control her life – one morning during a street preaching rally Susan decides she has had enough. Her father confronts her and she storms out of the family home and sets out for foreign shores.

Susan is shipwrecked during a cross ocean voyage. She surfaces on a floating island of trash. She scours the island in a desperate attempt to survive but soon discovers that her ability to tell reality from delusion is sorely tested as the island opens her eyes to the ways of the world.

She is befriended by Bal a dispossessed, nationless man trying to set up his own nation on the island with the help of Nazreen a botanist intent on creating a new utopian state from the refuse of the Western world.

As Susan compares the life she had and the hardships survived by those around her she grows and changes, however this does not mean that she embraces her father's point of view, she just grows to understand it.

She is rescued by a TV documentary team and for a very brief moment is a celebrity, trying to preach an ecology message but Susan soon learns that the world tires quickly and doesn't want to be told how to live. She and her father are reunited but on her terms.

NOTE

This piece can be performed in a number of different ways depending on scale, budget and in the case of 'the creatures' artistic tastes and imagination. As I see it the creatures can be performed by puppets (small, large or huge) or by living actors (and a combination of both); I'm sure projection of CGI characters is also possible but let's stick to solids as they just carry more weight and cost less.

Although realism is certainly not a prerequisite to the piece, the reality of Susan's dire situation should never be questioned. Although it is never clear whether Susan is seeing real creatures of those conjured by exhaustion or bio-hazard poisoning – it should be remembered that they are always real to her.

THE SET – A mere suggestion

Trash Island is a literal character within the play – obviously based on the deplorable expanse of floating trash in the Pacific Ocean. It's a mixture of bottles and multi-coloured plastic debris. Although the mix is up to you I would suggest the more colours the better, however the following must be included a number of plastic ducks, plastic sheeting, and an up-turned plastic picnic table with only one leg. Other necessary trash props include a dead seagull and a trashy gossip magazine and a half empty easily identifiable plastic Coke bottle.

As the creatures and certain items are situated within the trash island, careful placement is occasionally needed and in others cases use of a trap door or obscuring lighting may be needed.

It occurs to me that a partially inflated stage may help to convey the buoyant, unsteady structure of Trash Island – in essence performing on a bouncy castle – this certainly is a daft idea and certainly isn't essential but that's the feel moving within the set should portray – obviously the cheapest method would be the old favourite, acting.

CHARACTERS

Note –

The roles of the Dock Workers, Tat, Drall, Buck and Richie, members of the press and brethren should / could all be played by the same cast members – Pastor Reynolds and Bal could also be played by the same cast member.

Preacher Reynolds

In his late fifties, a Pastor of a fringe Christian sect (although other sects are available). Not an intentionally cruel man but someone who feels lost and powerless in the modern world and therefore exerts his own power and fear over those he should be protecting with his love.

Susan Reynolds

19 and aching for an experience away from her smothering family. She takes a working passage on-board a cargo vessel. She is dangerously naïve and inexperienced.

Mark

Working hand / ordinary seaman on the cargo vessel – 24, a decent guy who's prefers working passenger vessels but will take whatever's going, long term plans include opening his own restaurant or failing that a bar probably in Cambodia.

Dock Workers / DRALL & TAT

The dock workers also play or voice the creatures. Born of Trash Island they may or may not be figments of Susan's fevered mind.

Bal

President King of the Island State of Trash, an exiled journalised, now a man without a nation, a dispossessed man who is trying make the best of it.

Nazreen

A Libyan refugee, citizen number two of the Island State of Trash, she is botanist trying to grow an island from the refuse of the world.

Buck

An American freelance journalist/ film maker, working on a yet unfunded documentary – he wants to sell his work to the National Geographic or the BBC.

Richie

Australian competitor to Buck – also freelance, looking to make it big with his next documentary.

Trash Island

OPENING: A dark stage – the sounds of a traffic and a busy street market.

Stage lights up (chair at far right in darkness). Pastor Reynolds, Susan and a small group of believers march onto the stage and form a group at the far left of the stage. The Pastor carries a small step ladder from which he preaches. They are all wearing overcoats and look too tidy, restrained and strangely out of their time – the women all have their head covered. One or two tambourines are present but this is not a 'Gospel' or 'Happy Clappy' group they are far more extreme and sullen – such as Exclusive Brethren. The Pastor climbs onto his stepladder.

PASTOR

Then the Lord said, "The outcry against Sodom and Gomorrah is so great and their sin is so grievous that I will go down and see if what they have done is as bad as the outcry that has reached me. Genesis 18 v20. God is good. It was the Son of God himself who walked those very streets of Sodom and Gomorrah in his immortal form, the son of God who saw and judged the sin of those towns. The very son of God who knowing the depravity and evil of mankind was born into the flesh, born of a virgin and died on a cross for our sins.

But brothers and sisters he will come again and he will judge. The word of |God tell us the sky will be folded up like a scroll and thrown away Revelation 6, v14. And Behold I saw a new heaven and a new earth for the former earth had passed away; Revelation 21, v1. A new earth will be created in the presence of God. God did not spare his own son to save us and his son did not spare Sodom and Gomorrah, and I say to you, no unrepentant sinner shall see the Kingdom of God. We now stand as his witnesses, witnesses to his light and the sin of the world and surely it will be condemned.

Fornication, blasphemy, the same abomination of depravity and lust that lived in the streets of Sodom and Gomorrah is alive and well here today…

A plastic bottle lands on the stage – sounds of derisive laughter.

PASTOR

Do not be surprised, for doesn't the good Lord himself tell us in Matthew 24, v9. You will be handed over and persecuted, hated by all nations, in my name. But the one who stands firm will be saved.

Susan looks increasingly self-conscious – insults are shouted from offstage. Susan storms away.

PASTOR

Susan! Susan come back here at once! *(She freezes)* Fear not when they mock and despise you! Fear not when they mock and persecute you! Stand in his name! Stand against the principalities and powers of this fallen nation. This nation of degradation! *(Susan walks to far end of stage)* Susan! Susan do not disobey me child, honour your Father and your Mother… Susan!

Susan takes off her coat and sits sullen and tense in the chair – she takes a mobile phone out of her pocket and puts an ear phone in one ear. Pastor Reynolds storms across the Stage and takes off his coat.

PASTOR

Susan! Susan! How dare you?! You disgraced me in front the congregation! What were thinking? Explain yourself. I'm waiting. Susan, I will not be defied by own daughter! Susan! What's that? Answer me, what is that in your ear?

SUSAN

It's an ear piece.

PASTOR

What is it?

SUSAN

I'm listening to the radio.

PASTOR

The radio. Are you listening to pop music?

SUSAN

No Father. It's Radio 4.

PASTOR

The world and all its filth. Have you forgotten what the word of God tells us, Listen to what is good, and edifying and holy.

SUSAN

No Father of course I haven't forgotten, how could I forget, it's the only thing I've ever heard since I was born.

PASTOR

Because you have been schooled in the ways of righteousness, brought up in the word of God. Let us pray Susan, let us pray that you find the strength…

SUSAN

No Father, no. You don't want me to be strong you want me to do what I'm told.

PASTOR

You will honour your Father and Mother so says the word…

SUSAN

Parents do not test your children.

PASTOR

I am not testing you Susan, the Lord is testing you. Will you find yourself wanting?

SUSAN

No Father, you are testing me, you're always testing me and I've had enough, I can't live like this.

PASTOR

A Minister who cannot control his own household is not worthy of honour!

SUSAN
So it's all about you.

PASTOR

Throw it away child, turn your back on the ways of the devil. Come out and be separate from them, so says the word of the Lord. Stop your backsliding and repent.

SUSAN

I'm listening to Radio 4 Father, Radio 4.

PASTOR

The works of the devil

SUSAN

Its Woman's Hour Father...

PASTOR

Sin and deprivation.

SUSAN

There's a world out there, a world of people and life and I want... I want to see it.

PASTOR

The Lord calls us to bear witness to his greatness... not to listen to the lies and pleasures of the world. The heart of man is wicked beyond all things child, will you be seduced by its works? Will you be shunned by the congregation of the Lord?

SUSAN

I don't know Father, will I, will I be shunned?

PASTOR

Repent and mend your ways, as the Lord said to the woman caught in adultery, go forth and sin no more.

SUSAN

I don't think that's possible.

PASTOR

With God's strength all is possible. Repent and be saved.

Susan stands and puts on her coat. The Pastor makes a grab for her coat. They tussle and he strikes her. Susan stands back from him and puts the chair between them.

PASTOR

I forbid you to leave. I forbid it. You will heed the word of your Father and obey or… I will cut you off.

SUSAN

Thank you Father. Between you and Woman's Hour I've learnt a lot this week. On Monday's program I learnt it's possible to sign on to a ship and work your passage across the world, you can see the world. As soon as I heard that… I knew I wanted to do it… and now… now I've learnt I can.

(Susan marches off stage. The Pastor stands silent. Raises his hand to heaven.)

PASTOR

Lord Father, test her in your fire so that she may be proved and made pure. Save her. Even though the flesh may be destroyed, save her soul. God is good.

STAGE To black - Sounds of a port. Waves, seagulls. The sounds become increasingly more industrial with machinery, and engines, the beeping of reversing vehicles. An ocean going cargo vessel is being loaded.

Lights rise on a dock yard – large boxes of galley supplies being tethered. Signs saying 'RESTRICTED AREA' and indicating 'HARD HATS MUST BE WORN AT ALL TIMES' abound. Two workmen (one male one female – she holds the checklist) in hard hats and visibility jackets are checking through the final manifest of essential supplies. Above them swings a tethered pallet.

Enter Susan – she is carrying a large backpack. She carries a passport and boarding pass in one hand. She is clearly lost and somewhat overwhelmed by the situation. She approaches the female worker.

SUSAN

Sorry, can you help me.

WORKER (TAT)

You shouldn't be over here this is a restricted area. It's not safe.

SUSAN

Sorry. I'm lost. I'm looking for The Varkum Rise.

WORKER (TAT)

I said this is a restricted area.

SUSAN

I'm signed on as crew. I'm work my passage on a boat called The Varkum Rise.

WORKER (DRALL)

They'll work your passage alright.

TAT

That's enough of that…and it's a freighter not a boat. Show me the boarding pass. *(Susan hands her a document.)*Right… it's this one here but you can't board here. You have to board there.

SUSAN

Thank you… (Moves off and is stopped)

TAT

Where you going?

SUSAN

You said over there.

TAT

Yes but you can't get over there by going through here, you have to go back over there. This is a restricted area.

DRALL

Unless you want to go on with the fresh meat? Basic
supplies only.

TAT

Report to the Harbour Masters Office and have your
papers checked.

SUSAN
But I just came from there…

TAT

So what are you doing here?

ENTER MARK – he is carrying a large duffle bag.

DRALL
Go on, clear off.

MARK
Hay what's the problem?

TAT

Oi this is a restricted area! Can't anybody read bloody signs?

MARK

Alright, hold your water. What's the problem Miss?

SUSAN

I've signed on to work my…I can't find my boat, freighter…

MARK
Ship

SUSAN

Right, The Varkum Rise…

TAT

I told her already, it's this one.

MARK

That's my ship too. So we're in the right place.

DRALL

No, this is a restricted area. You are in the wrong place.

MARK

Don't mind them. Every port has one, although twins are not uncommon. Would you like us to leave the area?

DRALL

At once.

TAT

If not sooner.

MARK

No problem. *(Takes Susan by her arm and attempts to walk past the workers.)*

DRALL

Woah, what you doing?

MARK

Leaving the restricted zone by the shortest route. Going over there.

TAT

I just told her you can't go through here to get over there.

MARK

Why not?

DRALL

Because we're here.

TAT

We're working here.

MARK

But that's where the crew are boarding, and we're the crew.

TAT

Go round.

DRALL

Go back.

TAT

You can't come through here.

MARK

Guys come on… here, there, stop, come, go. They're all concepts created to control the working man.

DRALL

No, they're rules created to stop you getting crushed into a wafer by a thirty ton crate.

MARK

Do you love me?

DRALL

Do what pal?

MARK

Do you even like me?

DRALL

Less and less.

MARK

Do you like my friend here…

DRALL

I don't know her.

TAT

I wouldn't mind giving her…

MARK

So you don't like me and you don't like her and you definitely don't want us to be here so… what do you care if we get hurt going over there.

TAT

Why don't you just fuck off?

MARK

I will…once I'm over there.

DRALL

Go on….piss off, go, go now…

TAT

What? No…

MARK

Just looking at that line. *(Points upwards)* That look alright to you.

TAT

It's fine.

MARK

The opposable thumb clamps all working today are they?

DRALL

What?

MARK

Your opposable thumb clamps all okay, you got the memo right? Are they all working like they should?

DRALL

I reckon.   We got the memo right.

TAT

Sure we did. It was about…

MARK

The risk of increased strain in the ninety degree opposable thumb clamps when using the overhead remote cranes.

DRALL

Yeah that was it. Yeah we got it covered.

MARK

Great…we'll get out of your way then.

TAT

This is a restricted area.

MARK

(To Susan) Come on, let's get you on-board. Bet you could do with a cup of tea.

SUSAN

Could I ever.

MARK

So where you from…

Susan and Mark exit stage – laughing and chattering to themselves.

DRALL

Wanker.

TAT

Yeah…I'd better check on that memo. Can't be too careful with those…posy thumbs right? *(She leaves stage left)*

DRALL

Right. I'll… *(Walks backwards, looking up, slowly walking off to the wings)* Looks fine to me. That's blokes talking bloody rubbish, nothing wrong with that posy…wanker. *(Exit)*

Ships siren – Mark and Susan stand together at the edge of the stage.

MARK

So first time on board a ship?

SUSAN

First time doing anything.

MARK

Really? I'd keep that to yourself if I were you.

SUSAN

Why?

MARK

Everything has a value.

SUSAN

What do you mean?

MARK

There's no point in making yourself a target… its best to look experienced. Even if you're not.

SUSAN

And how does that look?

MARK

Good question. Trust less and question more.

SUSAN

I want to question everything. Try everything.

MARK

Keep that to yourself too.

SUSAN

Should I trust you?

MARK

Not too much. But yes you can trust me.

SUSAN

Do you believe in guardian angels?

MARK

No, I don't.   Do you?

SUSAN

I do.

MARK

You know what…

SUSAN

Keep that to myself too?

MARK

I would. Here we go then…

SUSAN

An adventure, a great adventure…

MARK

Stick close to me okay.

SUSAN

Sure.

MARK

Wave.

They wave – stage to black – a ship's siren sounds.

(SOUND EFFECT: A HUGE STORM AT SEA – THUNDER – SCREAMING METAL – WIND - SIRENS).

Night – the sound of a storm at sea. Crashing waves, an increasing wind, quickening into a violent tempest. In the distance a light from a ship rises and falls as it's tossed around by the waves. There is the sound of a siren – thunder, lightning - the ship's light swings out across the audience and then dies. The storms settles as the stage lights rise and Trash Island is revelled.

Lights up on Trash Island, a multi-coloured, shinning, wet, endless expanse of plastic trash.

Silence.

A hand breaks through the trash. Gasping for air. Susan attempts to climb through the trash. At first she struggles and sinks from sight. Rises again coughing and spluttering – with great effort she lays across the trash and pulls herself free of it as if from quicksand. Susan is dressed in a wet and ruined party dress (a floral print – pretty but not expensive), she has lost both shoes and her make-up is a water washed mess. She tries to stand, but the island is very unsteady and she falls to her knees and nearly sinks into the trash again. She sees an upturned floating plastic garden table, three of its legs are broken off.

She swims, crawls, rolls over to it and finally stands shivering and soaked upon its unsteady surface– overcome by the exertion – she curls up into a ball.

Lights dim – the sound of the sea increases – Susan begins to dream. We hear Mark's voice full of terror scream "Susan!"

The lights immediately rise as Susan sits bolt upright – thinking she has heard Mark she jumps to her feet nearly toppling the table.

SUSAN

Mark! Mark.   Mark. Please.

She dumbly views the scene. She turns and turns. She whimpers, shivers.

.

SUSAN

Hay! Hay!   Help! Help!

The silence bears down on her. She hides her head in her hand. Stifles a scream, holds back tears. Again Susan turns and turns about looking for another survivor. She tries to see to the end of the island but it seems to be endless. She begins to shiver.

SUSAN

Think…think…cold. Got to make fire. *(Looks at plastic – picks up two random pieces and tries rubbing them together – drops them)* Maybe just get dry.

(Susan takes off her dress, her underwear doesn't match, and lays her dress out on the table.)

SUSAN

Colder. Not good.

She looks around sees some plastic sheeting some way off and contrives how to reach it. She moves to the edge of the

*table and reaches out but the sheet is still out of reach. She
tentatively reaches one leg out onto the island, tries to
gather her balance, takes another step, nearly falls,
balances, grabs the plastic sheet with her finger tips – and
then skips back to the pallet. She instantly wraps the
sheeting around herself and sits shivering on the table.*

SUSAN

Oh that's so much better.

*She stands and again surveys the scene. She screams not
from fear but frustration. And then gathers the plastic
sheeting around herself and covers her head.*

SUSAN

Should have watched those survival programmes with
Dad. *(Thinking of her parents chills her – she uncovers
her head.)* You reap what you sow ah Dad...all I need now
is a whale to swallow me whole and...cold...this is no
good.

*Behind her the huge tail of a whale emerges showering a
rain of trash down upon her. She turns sees the tail sink
into the trash. Susan reacts – sees the whales tail sink back
into the sea – pure panic. Falls back into trash and climbs
out, whimpering.*

Susan wrings out her dress, slips it back on and then wraps the plastic back around herself. She looks up at the sun, it's not yet high in the sky.

SUSAN

Cup of tea anyone.

Moving to the edge of the table she looks out for plastic bottles. There are many. She lifts one, its empty, another is half full but the cap is off so its sea water, another has its red cap on and is almost half full with a brown liquid. She eyes it suspiciously. Takes off the cap and sniffs – it's almost putrid – she braces herself and then tastes. She manages to keep it down with a struggle – looks at the bottle – braces herself and then downs the lot. Spits, gags, and nearly vomits.

SUSAN

Oh my God. Not nice, not nice. If that was the real thing I'm….ugh.

(Looks at the empty bottle)

That was stupid.

(She hurriedly checks for more bottles but all are empty or full of sea water.)

Better hope it rains then…without becoming a storm…oh God I'm so fucked.

A thoughts occurs to her – how deep is the trash? Could she possible fish? She stills her head into the trash, pulls it out, sticks in her right arm – doesn't feel water.

Deep…okay so I just need a rod right, a long rod.

In a burst of purposeful activity – she stands, drops the plastic sheeting, pulls off the last table leg, then removes her bra from under her dress, ties one strap to the table leg, looks at the other end – (thinking "hook?) – a momentary pause.

SUSAN

Hook…how to make a hook? And bait…bait. *(Picks up a random piece of plastic)* You look like a goldfish…maybe a fish finger…that's been run over by a speedboat. *(She tosses the piece of plastic behind her. She snatches back her bra in frustration and puts it on again from under the plastic sheet, then tears off the plastic sheet, increasing rage and throws it overboard.)*

Idiot! Bloody, bloody…idiot.

(She is on the edge of panic – tears well-up – put she force herself to be still. Wipes her eyes and then with great control wraps the plastic sheeting around herself.)

Okay twat enough twating about. Think about surviving…
(*Looks at empty Cola bottle*) Right so the basics of
survival…food. None. Shelter…hardly…water…too
much. None of it drinkable. So you better get rescued
quick. I need a signal…fire. I have to make fire.

(*She picks up two plastic bottles. Tries rubbing them
together. And looks at them fiercely.*)

What about a lens then? (*Working as she talks*) Get enough
bottles. Clean them. Make a magnifying lens and then
make a fire. This stuff is sure to smoke a lot, they'll see it
for miles. Make a fire, make a fire…in the middle of the
sea… (*She looks doubtful.*) Burning, melting plastic…lots
of burning plastic…with me in the
middle…equals…instant toxic barbeque. (*She looks
around her.*) So that's a no to the fire but I do need to
make a signal. Why didn't I watch Blue Peter, Art Attack
or…mission fucking impossible. Okay…get creative.
Think big…big words, big letters, one word
saying…HELP! (*Shouts*). All made out of different
coloured plastic bottles and stuff. Yeah I could do that.
Make a big HELP someone will see it and…how long will
it take? Depends on the letters…okay. It's a plan. Right.
So no time to waste.

*With an armful of bottles she sets about trying to form the
H for her hopeless plan. There follows a brave but futile
piece of slapstick which is to look akin to trying to juggle
oiled snakes whilst balancing on an and electric fence –*

her struggle to remain upright, fails but she gets up and gets up and gets up and then the sound of a helicopter sweeps overhead and then whirls away.

SUSAN

Hay! Hay! Over here, down here, down….you…! You…I'm down here…you bastard. Don't go! Don't go! *(She sinks to her knees – and then starts throwing trash up in the air in frustration)* Stupid flash bastard. You came too soon…too soon…typical bloody man. *(Begins laughing in desperation)* I'm so fucked.

(Susan looks to her left. She picks a mass from the trash – it is a sea bird, fetid, dead with a plastic bag stuck over its head.)

And there goes my appetite. *(She sniffs it)* Yep long gone.

(She drops the bird – to her right she finds a water logged cheap magazine – she holds it by her finger tips – the gently tries to turn the pages.)

I don't believe it… I've read it.

(She drops it – she thinks – picks it up puts it over her head and holds it on as a hat – then rolls swims over the trash back to the table.)

I need to build a boat and get my sorry arse out of here. A raft, that's all I need a raft and a paddle. This shit already floats so I've just got to bind some of it together…and go…get clear of this crap and then… then maybe they'll see me. If not I head for shore…or at least somewhere else. I've got to get out into the open. Okay…okay. It's a plan. Good plan.

(A few moments of fevered inaction – and then she slumps exhausted.)

Need to eat, need to get my strength…need fuel.

(She takes the magazine off her head, rips out a page, tears it in two and then in four pieces and shoves one piece and chews and swallows)

Really needs a nice Chardonnay, or a cider, cup-a-soup…ketchup.

(Eats another piece)

Roughage…plenty of roughage. So how to build a boat, or a raft?

(She slaps the table firmly and decisively)

It's a good plan.

DRALL (voice)

It's a plan.

(Susan turns quickly to see where the voice came from and falls off the table.)

SUSAN

Who said that…who said that?

DRALL (voice)

Flotsam and jetsam all.

SUSAN

Who said that? Where are you? Show yourself!

DRALL (Voice)

Flotsam and jetsam am I.

SUSAN

Come on where are you…show yourself…

Drall rises from the trash. He is a huge misshapen mass of refuge and litter. It moans and creaks as it stretches to its full height.

SUSAN

Are you the devil?

DRALL

Just a bit.

SUSAN

Get thy behind me Satan

DRALL

Really…does that make any sense? I mean if I was the devil would you really want me where you couldn't see me…would you?

SUSAN

What are you?

DRALL

Flotsam and jetsam am I. A mishmash of the discarded, son of accident, mishap and carelessness without a plan but full of intent.

SUSAN

Is that right? And what might that intent be?

DRALL

To live, to survive, mere whimsy really.

SUSAN

I'm going crazy, I'm talking to a pile of talking trash.

DRALL

You're only crazy if the trash answers back.   Oops. Oh dear.

SUSAN

Does my hallucination have a name?

DRALL

I am called Drall.

SUSAN

Drall…well that makes no sense.

DRALL

I am detritus, the debris of want.

SUSAN

And that still doesn't make any sense.

DRALL

Can you see rhyme or reason in the refuse of our being?

SUSAN

You sound like a preacher.

DRALL

I am your hallucination am I not?

SUSAN

I think you are a figment of my imagination or a head injury. Probably shouldn't have drunk that Coke...I've never had it before...I don't know what it's meant to taste like...it could have been anything...

DRALL

Microbes, burgeoning life waiting to be released. People do put strange things into bottles. Not just bad poetry.

SUSAN

You are not real and I refuse to focus on you any longer...I need to get on. I'm going to build a raft and get out of here. Are you going to stop me?

DRALL

No. Why would I? But first you should eat. Breakfast is the most important meal of the day. You should eat.

SUSAN

Do you have some food?

DRALL

Do we have some food? We have a mighty menu, a plentiful store, all the goodness of the sea. Seabass, crabs, crayfish, tuna, dolphin, shark all smothered in plastic particles.

SUSAN
I'll think I'll pass.

DRALL

A delusional side dish to go with the non-existent meal then...

SUSAN
I'm being tortured by an illusion.

DRALL

The kitchen is slow tonight but the pantry is full.
Misshapen sea creatures of all varieties, the hermit crab
who's made his home in a yoghurt pot, or the turtle that's
grown to look like the figure eight thanks to the plastic
binding wrapped around its shell: we do a truly splendid
Mock Styrofoam Turtle stew.

SUSAN

Is this a guilt trip? My hallucination is trying to put me on
a guilt trip. I didn't do this? I've never participated in
anything worldly. This is nothing to do with me.

DRALL
Old bikes, old clothes, tissues and pens and lost socks and
sanitary products.

SUSAN
That's a bit personal.

DRALL

That's is just the way it is...and we cannot change it. We
are in this world and we are of it. We are what you made
us.

SUSAN

I didn't do this.

DRALL

No blame, no shame. We all came here through the drain.

SUSAN

I once read a Friends of the Green something leaflet...and
now I really wish I hadn't. You are that leaflet...there is
more moral outrage than flesh to you Jacob Marley. Go
haunt someone else.

(DRALL sinks back into the trash – laughing as he goes)

SUSAN

Okay, okay...stop thinking, shut up and be
practical...raft...use the table....plastic sheeting for a sail.
(Gets busy collecting) Mast, I need a mast....or maybe just
a paddle. I must be able to make a paddle. Wrap the plastic
sheeting around some bottles, use the leg or...I could swim

out holding onto the wreckage...swim out into the Pacific Ocean.... Which is big, really, really big.

(She lowers herself into the trash – hold onto the table and kicks, harder and harder, then kneels on the trash and tries to push the table – nothing happens – she throws herself on to the table and screams in frustration.)

That was really dumb. I'm so hungry.

(She jumps to her feet – skips across the trash and retrieves the dead bird – again she sniffs it- opens her mouth.)

You can do it, you can do it, its chocolate covered, chocolate covered...pollution fouled dead stinking carrion.

(She throws it far away. Slowly she returns to the table, she holds a plastic bottle)

I'm going to have to drink my own urine. I'm going to have to drink my own piss. Oh god...

(She looks at the top of the bottle.)

Well that's not going to work. Need something a bit more.

(She inspects the plastic sheeting)

Oh Lord I could really do with a miracle....change water into...water. Piss into lemonade?

(She attempts to squat above the plastic sheeting she leans forwards – tries to see between her legs and topples off of the table and into the trash – she spits and scrambles and

*climbs back on – seemingly spitting and wiping her eyes –
she squeals with displeasure, frustration and disgust. A
low rumbling laugh echoes across the island)*

DRALL (voice)

I thought pride comes before a fall, not idiocy.

SUSAN

Come on then hallucination. Let's have you.

(Drall rises)

SUSAN

So now you have an ecumenical point to raise? A question
of faith. You know as hallucinations go, you're pretty
predictable.

DRALL

Do I remind you of anyone?

SUSAN

Don't think I haven't heard of Freud, I'm not a complete
idiot.

DRALL

I am what you made me. Please feel free to vent…

SUSAN

Yeah why not, seeing as we're here… Dad I want to thank you for making me go to Sunday school, and Wednesday prayer group and Friday bible study and making me stand on street corners every other Saturday. I want to thank you for no T.V after six, no mobile phones, no magazines and no skirts above the knee. You Victorian, cold hearted bastard, you drove me out of my home and put me here...the middle of the bloody ocean. Trying to get away from you brought me here… and now I miss you and I hate you for that…

DRALL

It's always somebody else's fault isn't it. Put on your big girl knickers and get on with it. But what do I know… I am the detritus of time and slime, toys and trash…

SUSAN

Enough with the Eco psychobabble. Help me. I need food. I need to food.

DRALL

But of course, it is an honour to serve.

(Drall points to a spot to the right of the table. Susan moves to the other side of the table and peers down into the trash, she can't make out what she is seeing, she frantically throws trash away to clear a space and then staggers back in horror)

DRALL

(Laughs) Does it not please you? Does it not meet your needs?

(Susan plunges her arms into the trash and pulls a human arm and shoulder on to the table.)

SUSAN

Its Mark isn't it. I know its Mark… we only met three days ago. He was sweet.

DRALL

Tasty sweet. Good enough to eat?

SUSAN

No. Never.

DRALL

But you must if you are to survive.

SUSAN

Never.

TAT *(- female voice only - a loud mocking laugh)*

What did I tell you?

Tat rises from the debris behind the table – she is slightly smaller but otherwise composed of the same debris as Drall.

TAT

Waste not want not.

DRALL

If that were true my love where would we be?

TAT

I consumed turtles and dolphins and fish before I was even born. I don't see why she should turn so green when it comes to eating one of her own. Too rare for you is it, a little underdone?

SUSAN

I can't eat him. He was…this is insane…

TAT

Turning down a free meal. That's insane.

SUSAN

I won't do it.

DRALL

We promise not to look.

TAT

You can promise all you like. I want to watch. You try strangling a shoal of jellyfish and see how it makes you feel, then you can talk to me about hard choices. Just eat him. Who's going to know?

SUSAN

I'd know.

DRALL

Just a finger or two. It would give you such strength for the task ahead.

TAT

And it seems such a shame to waste it. It won't stay fresh for long.

DRALL

Time and tidemark wait for no man.

TAT

Eat up before it gets cold. There's a good girl.

SUSAN

He was a friend. I liked him.

TAT

You'll like him just as much as lunch.

DRALL

It's what he would have wanted.

SUSAN

Stop it.

TAT

Here comes the chew, chew train…chew, chew. Into the tunnel we go…

DRALL

See this situation for what it is…the inevitable act of consumerism.

SUSAN

Shut up.

DRALL

It's an act of love really…him giving himself to you.

TAT

Be rude not to. Chow down.

(Susan knells – lifts Marks hands to her mouth – stops – balks – and then slowly pushes it back into the trash.)

TAT

Stop that…we can use that…waste not want not.

DRALL

We have learned the art of recycling.

TAT

I'm 80% percent recycled myself. Twenty percent organic, but I'm trying to cut back.

DRALL

Your heart is pure plastic my love.

TAT

He says the sweetest things. You cast-off you.

DRALL

You wreckage.

TAT

Driftwood.

DRALL

I love it when you talk dirty.

TAT

That's what we call trash talk.

(Both laugh hard and long – as they stumble and fall – Susan looks on – the creatures laugh themselves into silence and then look at Susan)

TAT

Suit yourself then.

DRALL

You're not eating your dinner…Manna from heaven, you know the story it won't keep, you can't let it go to waste.

SUSAN

I won't eat him… I don't need to… I'm not an animal.

TAT

Think, think, think, there's an idea in there.

SUSAN

I don't need to… something else will. Bait, he can be bait. *(Starts removing bra from under dress)* All I need to do is fish, I can make a rod and use him bait and then I'll be fine, I'll be fine…

DRALL

It's a plan.

TAT

But you know the problem with the plan don't you.

SUSAN

I don't know… *(Sticks her arm into the trash trying to feel the bottom of it)* I don't know how deep the trash goes…

TAT

And…

SUSAN

And?

DRALL

How are you going to bait your hook? Which bit of him goes first? And how are you going to…get it on the hook.

TAT

Use your pearly whites.

DRALL

Oh, the shark, babe, has such teeth, dear
And it shows them pearly white
Just a jackknife has old MacHeath dear,
And he keeps it out of sight

TAT

(Theme to Jaws) Duh Dum Duh Dum Duh DUM

SUSAN

I have a family. My Mum will be worried sick.

DRALL

No they won't, they'll be praying. Offering your body up so that your soul might be saved.

SUSAN

This will destroy my Mum.

TAT

Didn't stop you setting off across the globe did it. Should have thought of that before you went shooting off across the globe. Getting mixed up in God knows what…dirty, dirty girl.

DRALL

You'll never get home. You'll never see them again.

TAT

Poor Mummy.

SUSAN

I can do it. All I need to do is get away from this trash away from you.

TAT

Well that's nice.

DRALL

Out there alone in the ocean, adrift without food or water. How long will you last?

TAT

One good storm, that's how long.

DRALL

Why throw your life away?

TAT

Like so much…

SUSAN

Fish food.

TAT

It doesn't have to be that way.

DRALL

Flotsam and jetsam. Debris to debris, particle to particle, return to the trash that you created, in the sure hope of everlasting…

TAT

Non-biodegradable

DRALL

CFC free…life.

MARK

(Rises from the trash he covers himself in a robe of plastic – crowns himself with a plastic bottle – holds a plastic duck in one hand as Drall and Tat bow)

I am the Alpha and the Omega 3, the beginning and the end, I come to bring new life, new life.

DRALL & TAT

He is risen

MARK

For he that dies in me shall never know death but have instead eternal renewal. For I am the resurrection and the recycling, for ever and ever, for in my father's house there are many macerators, wouldn't I have told you if it wasn't so…unless I didn't want you to know.

SUSAN

Stop it! Stop it!

MARK

And the first shall be last. And who is the least of these shall be as my brother…and who is the least of these my creatures?

DRALL & TAT

We are, we are for we are flotsam and jetsam, trash upon the waves, the discarded and the disappointed. We are sins of the world.

MARK

And your sins shall be forgiven you. You shall be as white as snow. And woe to them that would hurt the least of my children, for it would be better for them that a millstone be tied around their necks and cast into the sea.

DRALL

And they shall be as bread cast upon the waters.

TAT

And we shall gobble them up and break them down and recycle and rebuild and be reborn. The true masters of the world. Servants of the one true god that consumes all.

MARK

And there shall be a new heaven and a new earth, a new Adam and Eve and they shall eat of the tree of others mistakes.

DRALL & TAT
Blessed are we! Blessed are we!

SUSAN

Stop it!

MARK

Susan why so glum? You know it's nothing but fun. Just a touch of sun stroke and sepsis, just those free radicals running wild, poisoning your brain and turning it to pulp. Lighten up girl, live a little. Come dance the plastic fantastic with me. *(Starts to sing)* I am sailing, I am sailing, stormy waters to be near you…

SUSAN

Get away from me…you're not real, you're not real.

MARK

(Moving towards Susan – as if walking on water)

Oh thee of little polyurethane. Taste and see, for I am the paste of life, taste and see that I am good. *(Mark offers her his hand and then slumps into her lap, dead)*

SUSAN

God *(Puts his hand to her mouth and bites)*

DRALL

And as it was foretold, so it has come to pass.

TAT

You made the mess now clear it up.

The sound of thunder – the sky darkens and lightning fills the sky – as the sound of a storm rises the stage darkens –

total darkness – waves rage – lights come up as the sea calms. Stage – Susan is alone, slumped on the table. Dry mouthed and fading fast.

The sound of tuneless whistling – Enter Bal on large homemade water skies striding over the trash. Bal sees Susan and rushes towards her. He gives her water from one of the many water bottles around his neck.

BAL

Come on sweetie drink, drink there's a good girl. Drink.

SUSAN

Are you real…

BAL

I am Bal. From Mogadishu. And you are?

SUSAN

Sue from England, the U.K.

BAL

EN – GA – LAND! The land of my dreams. Manchester United. The Beatles and The Radiohead. Fancy meeting you here, me old cock.

SUSAN

You're real, you're really real. How did you find me? Do you have a boat?

BAL

A boat no, no boat, skies. My very own design. Chocolate? *(He hands her a bar of milk chocolate)*

SUSAN

Food. *(Eats hungrily)* How did get this?

BAL

I trade with fishermen, water for plastic ducks and Lego, everybody loves Lego and there's a billion pieces floating in the sea… have you seen any grey eight piece segment blocks? Must be grey, Star Wars models are very popular, extra water for the original series.

SUSAN

You have contact with the outside world, that's brilliant, can you reach them?

BAL

Not exactly, we meet every six months or so, we pass, we trade, I traded this morning, the Millennium Falcon for water and two hundred Snicker bars. A good deal. Unfortunately I have a nut allergy.

SUSAN

That's pretty unlucky…

BAL

I am Bal the unlucky President King of the Island State of Trash. Were you on that ship that sank in the storm? So you are unlucky too. Welcome to the land of the unlucky. You are most welcome. *(Hands Susan a piece of cardboard)* Here you are, citizen number three.

SUSAN

What is this?

BAL

Passport.   You are now official citizen of Trash Island, southern district. As your President I offer you free health care and low taxes. Do you have a favourite song? We need a national anthem. *(Bal sees body part)* Was he also on the ship?

SUSAN

Yes…he was a friend of mine.

BAL

Unlucky friend.   Have you been eating him?

SUSAN

No I have not.

BAL

Are you going to eat him?

SUSAN

No I am not.

BAL

Good, it's against the constitution… and very bad for the
constitution. That is our national joke.

SUSAN

Bal where do you live?

BAL

A President King must live where he is… No not living,
ruling. I am a displaced person, a stateless man. So I find
myself in dis place in person and what a state I'm in.
(Laughs) That is our second national joke, it is a little
racist but so are all national jokes. Bal walks into a bar, the
barman says, why the long face, Bal says I live on an
island of Trash…it loses a lot in translation.

SUSAN

How did you get here? Where you shipwrecked too?

BAL

No I was thrown overboard by pirates. None of whom
looked like Johnny Depp. But Johnny Depp is still our
patron saint, mostly due to his work with Tim Burton and
his friendship with the late great Hunter S. Thompson, a
truly wild spirit. President Nixon sucks, President Reagan
sucks, President Clinton…well we all know about him.
War Pigs! Do the drugs, take the ride, do the drugs, write
the book...

SUSAN

Sounds… perfectly delightful.

BAL

I'm sorry Susan. I'm not used to talking to living people. I have talked to many drowned people in the last three years… and on the whole, I find them very receptive to my brand of humour.

SUSAN

Three years, you've been here three years. Haven't you tried to escape?

BAL

Escape, where would I go? I am a non-person.

SUSAN
You must have a family, people that miss you…

BAL

Not anymore. I was a journalist in my own country, the Hunter S. Thompson of Mogadishu. Perhaps you read my big exposé, Fear and Loathing in Mogadishu.

(Susan shrugs)

No…it went something like this, the President sucks, the government sucks… it didn't work out so well for my family. I spoke truth unto power…they don't like it.

I had to leave my own country. I became a migrant worker but there was no work for loud mouth journalists, so I became a refugee… and then of course nobody wanted me. I turned to people traffickers, who took me half wy and then…turned me into refuse…but now I am President of Trash Island. And things are looking up… in the last twenty four hours our population has increased by a third. Perhaps you would like to be Minister for the Environment. *(Laughs)* You could have a hat. *(Puts trash on her head)*

SUSAN

I want to go home.

BAL

Does home want you?

SUSAN

Of course, I have… I have a life.

BAL

What do you do? What is your chosen career path?

SUSAN

I haven't chosen yet.

BAL

So! Go into politics, Minister of Defence, we have a serious border problem... we haven't got one.

SUSAN

Thanks but... I might not have much of a life but it's mine and it's only just starting and... I'd like to get back to it.

BAL

No problem, we are a very tolerant nation, and have a complete freedom of movement policy... you can leave anytime you like.

SUSAN

Great...

BAL

England is eight thousand miles that way. *(Laughs)* I hope you have a boat, a plane or very strong arms.

SUSAN

You know I don't.

BAL

Welcome to your new home!

SUSAN

What about ships? I saw a helicopter, they must be looking for survivors?

BAL

That will be the documentary team, we get a lot of them. BBC, CBS, the Discovery Channel. We make good TV slots.

SUSAN

So rescue is possible, we've just go to make contact with them and get me…

BAL

Girl, you've been thrown away… you are citizen of a country made of the world's trash… the world does not want to know the mess its making, it is not good TV.

Dying dolphins is good TV... trash and dying people not so much.

SUSAN

It sounds like brilliant TV to me. I need to find these TV crews, where are they?

BAL

On a boat, beyond our borders... they are not my concern.

SUSAN

Will you help me?

BAL

I am a very busy man, I have my official duties.

SUSAN

Bal come with me, I need you. Please... I promise I'll do everything I can to get you into my country. I'll tell them you rescued me, you saved my life. They'll listen, they'll take you in...

BAL

One voice against the fear of the dark stranger, you know nothing of the world.

SUSAN

I'll make sure you're alright…

BAL

Your world threw me away. They wanted nothing to do with me… I return the favour. I am President King of the wild frontier.   But I will call Nazreen. She may feel differently…

SUSAN

And who's Nazreen?

BAL

(Builds a huge flag out of trash from his water skies – and produces a Aboriginal Bull Horn - also made out of trash)

She is the other third of our fluctuating population. She's around here somewhere, unless she drowned last night. If she hasn't drowned we must be very careful… if she has drowned be just as careful, she's a very tricky person…with very questionable personal hygiene. I have two citizens…one is a rebel and one wants to leave, society is falling apart.

(He swings the Bull Horn – an eerie sound reverberates over Trash Island)

SUSAN
What shall I do?

BAL

I don't know…pick up some trash… *(Laughs)* That's…

SUSAN

I know, it's your national joke.

(Lights dim – evening falls)

ACT 2

Lights rise on a new day. Susan is asleep on her raft. Bal is still swinging the Bull Horn –

NAZREEN

(Voice off stage) Alright, alright, I can hear you, *(Enters stage- pulling a heavily loaded bright orange dinghy)* never a minutes peace, as soon as you sit down somebody's calling you. Right, what do you want now?

BAL

Now? What do you mean now? I haven't seen you in three months… this is hardly demanding behaviour.

NAZREEN

Moan, moan. I came here to get away from red tape, enough of your bureaucracy, what do you want?

BAL

Nazreen, Susan; citizen number three – *(Aside to Susan)*
'Don't shake hands.' Susan, Nazreen Sanjarani, Minister
for Infrastructure.

SUSAN

Bal says you can take me the film crew that have the
helicopter?

NAZREEN

Does he now? And why would I do that?

SUSAN
I'm trying to get home.

NAZREEN

But you've only just arrived? Is it the climate? The never
ending evidence of man's indifference to his environment.
The lack of sexual gratification?

 I don't know. The TV crew are over there in the South,
two or three day's journey, I've already done that sector.
It's going to play havoc with my schedule. I'm already
behind… No I'm sorry, I can't…

BAL

No, no,no my dear Minister, you don't have to take her, just call them, get them here.

SUSAN
You've got a phone.

BAL and NAZREEN laugh

NAZREEN

That's right, we're totally wireless here, Wi-fi

BAL

Broadband! *(They fall into silence)* Of course she can pay, I have been feeding her nutritious Snicker bars and fresh water, and to my knowledge she has yet to expel any waste. Here's the deal. We call the journalists, who are always full of shit, this I know for certain, we all gather... we eat Snickers we...you collect. It would take a lot of work off your hands.

NAZREEN

I don't know those TV types are so unpredictable. Are you regular?

SUSAN

I don't know what you mean…

NAZREEN

This is no time to be coy. Your bowel movements, your passing of stools, are you regular?

SUSAN

I'm feeling the need more and more these days.

BAL

And she has a friend…meet Mark, grade one fertiliser.

NAZREEN

A floater… fantastic.

NASREEN

Perhaps we can come to some arrangement. I call the TV bods tonight after you deliver… as a sign of goodwill and in return I get the floater, plus all available nutrients. Deal?

SUSAN

I'm not sure what I'm agreeing to?

BAL

It is Nazreen's infrastructure project, that's all you need to know.

NASREEN

Are you mad, the whole world needs to know, and you, you must tell them…that's the other part of the deal, tell them what we are trying to achieve out here. Get me seeds, and manure, lots of manure. I've tried talking to those TV guys and… very narrow minded people, very square…square TV minds.

BAL

Pigs.

SUSAN
Okay sure but… what am I agreeing to exactly… and what do you want with Mark?

NAZREEN

The same I want with you. Fertiliser.

BAL

It may have escaped your notice but we are a nation without trees or any noticeable flora or fauna. And you cannot be an officially recognised island without flora or fauna.

NAZREEN

So I'm planting seeds.

SUSAN

In plastic?

NAZREEN

No in shit.   (Pause)

SUSAN
Oh I see....nutrients...What if it doesn't float?

NAZREEN

In bowls, milk cartoons, bottles, balloons, buckets, has it escaped your notice we have a lot of plastic around here? Shit in bowls, do you think I'm an idiot?

SUSAN

No…no I don't think that.

NAZREEN

Its basic hydroponics. And island building. The plants
grow, their weeds bind together, which binds the plastic
together. The plastic gathers passing dust and earth. Insects
come and they attract birds, birds drop seeds and soon we
have more plants, more growth, very soon we have an
island teeming with life… science.

SUSAN

Sure I'll…go in a bucket for that.

NAZREEN

Yah! We have a deal. *(Hands her a dirty white bucket)*
You get to it, and I'll deal with our friend here. *(She pulls
an axe from her dinghy)*

SUSAN

What? O…you can't I won't let you…

NAZREEN

But I have to. He's no use to anybody like he is,., but I could turn him into something really useful… compost for vines, nettles, ivy.. look I'll plant a rose bush if you like?

SUSAN

But why the axe? Why do you need the axe? Why can't you just plant it near him, over him?

NAZREEN

You have to open them up.

BAL

You really do need to open them up.

SUSAN
No you don't.

BAL

No you really do, otherwise they swell up.

NAZREEN

It's the gas. You've got to let it out.

BAL

Or they swell and swell and then… bang! Bits of stinky friend everywhere. It's not nice.

NAZREEN

A health hazard…and as Minister for Health, I won't allow it.

BAL

It has to be done.

SUSAN

But he was my friend.

NAZREEN

You don't have to watch. Did I say she had to watch? You don't have to watch. We're not without feelings… *(She removes a 'screen or instant tent' from the dinghy and puts it up around the body)* Would you like to say something?

SUSAN

Dear Lord… no, I don't think…this is Mark, my friend…I… thank you Mark for your friendship, it really was appreciated… I wish I'd got to know you better…and you'll be missed, I'm sure you'll be missed… I promise, if you have any family I'll let them know what a good man you were.

BAL and NAZREEN

Compost to Compost, life to life, grow something tasty, grow something nice.

SUSAN

Not good guys, not good.

NAZREEN

It's more than most get.

(She steps behind the screen – we see her in silhouette – she raises the axe and really goes to town – her bloody hand appears outside the screen)

NAZREEN

Rosebush!

(Bal hands her a rosebush from the dinghy – she plants the bush and appears from behind the screen, wiping her face. Bal and Susan look on in shock)

Right then… I've the 'Wi-fi' to prepare. And you've got a job to do. My blog, you log, I blog.

BAL

That is not a national joke.

Nazreen hauls a vast light from the back of her sledge - it seems to be constructed out of tinfoil and coloured plastic paper – as Bal plays drums on plastic pots and sings a very rough but heart felt version of "Coming in the air tonight" – the construction finishes –

BAL and NAZREEN

Have you been yet?

SUSAN

I can't when people are watching…

NAZREEN

Would you like some figs?

BAL

Prune Juice.

NAZREEN

A microbead enema?

SUSAN

No… I'll go when I'm ready.

NAZREEN

A deals a deal I call…when you answer the call.

They all stand around looking at nothing. Susan tuts and walks off stage.

BAL

You've changed your hair.

NAZREEN

I have, thank you for noticing, do you like it.

BAL

It's very you. Where did you find it?

NAZREEN

On an octopus.

BAL

The fact, that that doesn't shock me… is worrying.   Did it put up much of a fight?

NAZREEN

When don't they… we came to an arrangement. He had something I wanted… I had something he wanted… you know octopi, insatiable.

BAL

You are a very disturbing individual.

Susan walks back on stage and offers Nazreen the white bucket. Nazreen takes it, looks inside and smiles.

NAZREEN

Your Excellency is spoiling us.   A deals a deal.

She hits the light (stage to black) a beam of light swings across the island and the audience – not a 'bat signal' but a 'Tree Signal' appears in the sky. Bal, Nazreen and Susan settle down as the stars appear.

SUSAN

What now?

NAZREEN

We wait till morning…

BAL

We should all tell jokes, funny stories, like the time I mistook a condom for a jellyfish.

NAZREEN

That was a terrible meal.

BAL

I spy! I spy something beginning with…T.

NAZREEN

No it begins with P.

BAL

P?

NAZREEN

And rhymes with brick.

BAL

You are a very negative person.

NAZREEN

I wonder why?

BAL

Stories then to pass the time… come on, Susan what is
your story, why were you on that ship?

SUSAN

It's difficult to say now. My father is a Pastor, a preacher. I
was brought up in the church and… well… it was no life.
My father wanted me to be something I wasn't and … I
left home.

NAZREEN

Did he beat you?

SUSAN

It happened when I was little but…

BAL

My father used to hit me all the time. He had a special slipper called Maud, Maud the slipper. Do this Bal, BANG. Don't do that Bal BANG… but it was done with love.

NAZREEN

Love, you call hitting a child love. You don't hit the things you love… not unless they ask you to. And never children.

BAL

Compared to the Secret Police in Mogadishu, it was most lovely. I miss my father he was a good man.

NAZREEN

Good. What is good? My father never touched me… he was a completely useless man.

SUSAN

He hit me once, but I think he was as shocked as I was.

NAZREEN

He was a cruel man.

SUSAN

No but harsh, cold. He wanted to bring me up in a certain way.

BAL

He wanted to protect you.

NAZREEN

He wanted to control you.

SUSAN

Yes.

BAL

He wanted the best for you.

NAZREEN

He wanted to decide what was best for you.

SUSAN

Yes

BAL

He was a parent.

NAZREEN

He was a bad parent.

SUSAN

No… he could have done better.

BAL

He was human.

SUSAN

Yes, but he forgot that, he forgot he was human.

NAZREEN

Which is very human. Did he feed you? Clothe you? Care for you? Drive you around? Read you stories?

SUSAN

Yes he did those things too.

NAZREEN

And you got on a boat?!

BAL

Did you sing?   Did you sing in your church?

SUSAN

Of course…a bit.

BAL

I like singing, I think our national song should change every month, so we never get sick of it.

NAZREEN

I am sailing, sexy Rod Stewart.

BAL

Bridge Over Troubled Waters, Simon and Garfunkel

NAZREEN

The Tide is High, Blondie

BAL

Shelter from the Storm, Bob Dylan

NAZREEN

Don't Rock My Boat, Bob Marley.

SUSAN

I don't know any of those… I don't even know who they are.

NAZREEN

You don't know who Bob Marley is… throw her off the island at once. That is a new rule, nobody on the island who doesn't know Bob Marley…

BAL

No Nazreen, we must be inclusive... everybody coming onto the island must learn Bob Marley.

NAZREEN

You make an excellent politician... which isn't saying much.

BAL

What songs do you know?

NAZREEN

Yes 'Miss I don't know Bob Marley' who do you know?

SUSAN

Hymns.

BAL

Hymns.

NAZREEN

Well go on then, hymn. Let's hear one.

BAL

Yes go on sing, sing a hymn…

SUSAN

I can't think of any now…

NAZREEN

A water based hymn, with an island theme? If you can.

SUSAN

Okay…right.

Eternal Father, strong to save,
Whose arm hath bound the restless wave,
Who bidd'st the mighty ocean deep
Its own appointed limits keep;
Oh, hear us when we cry to Thee,
For those in peril on the sea!

NAZREEN

Now you see that there… that is a song.

BAL

That is hymn. We shall adopt it.

NAZREEN

Put in a reggae beat.

BAL

Right on sister… *(He starts drumming on plastic pots)*

THEY sing to the beat – gradually getting the words right.

Eternal Father, strong to save,
Whose arm hath bound the restless wave,
Who bidd'st the mighty ocean deep
Its own appointed limits keep;
Oh, hear us when we cry to Thee,
For those in peril on the sea!

(They laugh)

NAZREEN

Now it's a song!

BAL

Now it's a hit!

NAZREEN

Child, you must let go of your anger. It weighs too much.
It pulls you down. Your father, my father, all fathers are
mortal men, and like all men are full or errors… do not
weigh yourself down with anger over dust. Save your
anger for the men who do harm by choice, not those trying
to swim in the tide of life… let it go.

SUSAN

I'm not sure it's that easy.

NAZREEN

Nothing is easy until you do it.

BAL

Wisdom. Wise words and good counsel, yes this is the
stuff of life.

We should all huddle together and share our wisdom… in
order to keep warm.

NAZREEN

(Produces a knife) Men.

BAL

I'll sit over here. *(Moves away and settles down)*

NAZREEN

You do that. Don't mind him. I know he means no harm. But his feet stink.

SUSAN

How did you get here Nazreen?

NAZREEN

By boat.

SUSAN

No I mean what's your story?

NAZREEN

Have you heard of the ancient tribe of the Amazons?

SUSAN

I thought they were a myth.

NAZREEN

And so they are, but no one told my Father… well actually everybody told my Father but he didn't listen. He dragged me half way around the world and back again looking for his Amazon women. But one day in an airport in Brazil, I found a book called 'The Man who Planted Trees,' I loved this book, do you know it? It's about a man who walks the world…planting trees to build a forest… I decided if I ever had the chance I too would plant trees and build a forest. And then one day I found the Pacific trash island.

SUSAN

You mean you chose to come here?

NAZREEN

Not exactly. I was escaping the war in Libya. I was lucky I had a thousand American dollars, I then discovered that a thousand American dollars only gets you so far… it got me a boat, supplies and diesel but the diesel only got me to the middle of the Mediterranean… some fisherman found me and decided my boat was better than their boat…they forced a trade on me…they traded my boat for an inflatable rubber ring. I drifted to the shores of Greece. I was safe… until some unscrupulous Russian business men decided to offer me and six other woman work on their freighter… they did not want us to cook. You do what you have to do to survive. I survived for three weeks. *(Looks at knife)* I will never survive again. When we reached the pacific the Russians thought we'd survived long enough and threw us off the ship. The island found me… the other girls were not so lucky.

Susan and Nazreen huddle together and all three sleep, as they do DRALL AND TAT rise behind them menacingly. They take hold of Bal and Nazreen and drag them down into the trash (or off stage) – Morning comes – the sound of seagulls – Susan wakes to find herself alone.

SUSAN

Bal! Bal! Nazreen!

Susan tries to find a bottle of water but finds she is incredibly weak. She holds a bottle in her hand, she attempts to drink from it but it has been empty for days.

SUSAN

And Jonah ran from the will of God… and was swallowed by a whale…they went to see in a sieve they did and they went to see in sieve…with an owl and a pussy cat and plenty of honey, honey; lucky bastard owl…swallows and amazons…sorry Dad.

(She slumps forwards and then onto her back. The sound of waves and gulls continue. Drall and Tat slowly rise from the debris, they stand over Susan.)

DRALL and TAT

Eternal Father, strong to save,
Whose arm hath bound the restless wave,
Who bidd'st the mighty ocean deep
Its own appointed limits keep;
Oh, hear us when we cry to Thee,
For those in peril on the sea!

Mark rises from the trash – wrapped in plastic sheet and seem to shine and shimmer.

MARK

Trash unto trash, we deliver this thy servant back into the stew of life eternal and everlasting. Warranty, warranty where is thy sting, all things shall pass away and even this shall pass.

Mark produces a plastic doll and holds it like a baby in her arms, he holds it out to the world. DRALL shows it a rubber duck – the baby cries with a deafening blast like the sound of straining steel and grinding stone. The sound becomes the whirring of a helicopter. Mark, Drall and Tat exit merging with the trash.

Ropes drop from the sky and Buck and Richie descend. They slowly approach Susan.

BUCK

Have the gulls had a go?

RICHIE

Not that I can see. No, she's all in one piece. Poor kid.
Must have been on that freighter.

BUCK

You think she survived out here for three days?

RICHIE

She looks fresh.   Poor kid. *(Susan moves)* Jesus mate
she's alive.

(They rush to her)

BUCK

Ma'am, can you hear me, can you hear me, you're safe
now Ma'am, safe.

RICHIE

Get some water into her. She's got to be dehydrated. *(Into
radio to copter)* She's alive Jonesy, we need to get her out
of here quick. Let base know, she'll need medical
attention, she's burning up.

SUSAN

(Sits up) Bal?

BUCK

Take it easy Ma'am, your safe. We'll get you out of here
in a minute.

RICHIE

What's your name love?

SUSAN

Susan. Where's Bal, Nazreen?

RICHIE

Other survivors. (Looks around them) There's nobody
here.

SUSAN

You've got to find them, they were here, they saved me.
Nazreen called you.

BUCK

She's delusional. Just rest, you're safe now.

SUSAN

Nazreen called you, she built the light, you know Nazreen, she's planting the island.

RICHIE

Poor kid's gone nuts.

BUCK

Nobody called us, we were just passing, pure luck.

SUSAN

You know Nazreen.

BUCK

No we don't. You're dehydrated and confused. There's nobody else here.

Susan breaks away from them and franticly calls out for Bal and Nazreen, plunging her arms into the trash looking for them.

RICHIE

This isn't getting us anywhere mate. *(To copter)* Send down the winch we've got our hands full here.

Susan fights them, calling for Bal and Nazreen. A harness descends. They force her into it. Susan is lifted out. Calling for Bal.

BUCK

Hell of a story.   Better get her to sign some paperwork.

RICHIE

Exclusive rights.   We're gonna live out on this one mate.

Ritchie takes photos of Susan's exit and the island. Buck picks up the plastic baby doll.

BUCK

Could this be Bal… or Nazreen.

RICHIE

Could be. What's that…? *(Buck picks up Bal's water skies)*

BUCK

Must have come off that freighter. What's that…?

RICHIE

(Picks up a plastic bucket – sniffs it) You don't want to know… looks like somethings growing in it.

BUCK

She was one lucky girl. Another couple of hours and she'd be gull food.

RICHIE

No doubt about it. *(To radio)* Jonesy, we're ready to go mate. This place gives me the creeps.

BUCK

It's the end of the world. This is the future…

LIGHTS – OUT – THEME from THE NINE O'CLOCK NEWS – SOUND OF CROWDS. LIGHTS UP –

Buck and Ritchie are on stage (Buck is carrying a blanket).

BUCK

… and it stinks. Where she is?

RITCHIE

Give the girl a minute, this a big deal man…

BUCK

Don't I know it. You ready for this?

RITCHIE

Are you kidding me? Hello front page! Hello mini-series.

BUCK

We should really think about merchandise…

RITCHIE

Biodegradable.

BUCK

Right (Laughs) Here she comes... Susan you ready?

Susan enters dressed in jeans and t-shirt.

RITCHIE

You ready girl?

SUSAN

Sure... look I know I've already said this but, thank you, thank you for everything.

BUCK

The honour is ours... just one thing... would you mind putting this on?

RITCHIE

Just for the cameras.

BUCK

Can't have you looking too good.

LIGHTS DIM - CAMERA FLASHES – THE SOUND OF
CAMERAS – LIGHTS UP.

*Susan sits at a table centre stage wrapped in a blanket as
photographers mill around her, demanding pictures and
asking their questions all at once. Buck and Richie stand
behind her.*

BUCK

It was pure luck. We just happened to be passing getting
our last shots for an article we've been working on for the
National Geographic.

RICHIE

Life on the Pacific Trash Island.

BUCK

When we saw her, it was a close run thing for sure.

RITCHIE

We're just glad we were in time.

BUCK

Doesn't bear thinking about...

SUSAN

I was dying but Bal, he was refugee dumped by pirates, a journalist found me and gave me chocolate and then Nazreen, she was trying to make the island grow, creating new life, she called... I think the island took them, the island had created life... Mark was there...

BUCK

Obviously Susan has been through an awful lot and is still recovering.

RICHE

Mark was ship's hand on the freighter The Varkum Rise which was lost with all hands...

BUCK

Except Susan.

RICHIE

Three days before we found Susan…if we'd been a few hours more, maybe even minutes…there would have been no survivors at all. She's a very lucky girl.

BUCK

Now photos of our expedition and drinks are being served next door so… if you'd like to follow me.

More camera flashes – Buck and Richie walk off stage… "Funny thing about the Trash Island is its ability to draw the trash of the world into one place… its amazing what you find there, ducks, Lego, plastic dolls…" *the photographers follow – Susan is alone on stage at the table. She stands turns the table over and sits on it.*

(Pastor Reynolds enters and stands at the edge of the stage watching Susan – his hat in his hand – he is a humbled man)

PASTOR

Susan.

SUSAN

Hello Father… is Mum here?

PASTOR

She's waiting outside... too many people. And... I
wanted to see you first.

SUSAN

If you've come to gloat you can keep it.

PASTOR

No Susan, never.   I thank God for bringing you back to
me. When I did so much to drive you away. I thought I'd
lost you.

SUSAN

You did Dad.

PASTOR

Yes... but now?

SUSAN

You discarded me.

PASTOR

I was wrong. Full of pride.

SUSAN

How's the church?

PASTOR

I have found another church. I am no longer… a leader should be humble and deserving of respect, as was our Lord. I have learnt a lot… I ask you to…

SUSAN

They tell me I'm delusional because I believe I saw people on the island, monsters too. I can't accept that…which is what makes it a delusion… it feels a lot like faith… I know what I know… I believe but I can't prove anything. If you can't trust your eyes and you can't trust your head… and if you can't trust your family, what do you do?

PASTOR

You cast your bread upon the waters and see what comes back to you. Perhaps its how we treat one another that matters in the end… we are not the judges… thank God. It is not easy for a father to ask… but…

SUSAN

So don't. Don't ask.   You don't need to ask. I learnt a lot
too. Life's not so simple... like balloons. They bring so
much joy, and then we forget them... and then they choke
something else to death. Even the fun stuff has
consequences.

PASTOR

Will you come home?

SUSAN

No

PASTOR

Will you see your Mother?

SUSAN

Of course.   I don't have a problem with Mum.

PASTOR

I see... *(He weakens and turns to go)*

SUSAN

Will you buy a boat?

PASTOR

A boat? After all of this, you want to go back to sea?

SUSAN

I thought you liked fishermen?

PASTOR

Carpenters who are fishers of men.

SUSAN

Oh dear, so much for Sunday school. Are you only interested in lost souls? What are about the people wrapped around them?

PASTOR

Do unto the least of my people and you do unto me.

SUSAN

I always liked that one. Not easy though is it.

PASTOR

No he never said it was… but with God's strength …

SUSAN

No. Chocolate, water and a boat that's all we need…
chocolate, water and a boat…and maybe some seeds and
manure.

PASTOR

Manure…

SUSAN

To grow a land where all are welcome.

PASTOR

That's been tried, it never works out so well.

SUSAN

So we should give up?

PASTOR

Where would we get manure?

SUSAN

All God's children make it Daddy.

PASTOR

Some of us more than others...

SUSAN

Was that a joke?

PASTOR

When you realise how foolish you've been it is easier to joke.   What kind of boat do you want? A big boat?

SUSAN

Not really, as long as we've got an island base I think we could work something out.

PASTOR

God's children are not afraid of hard work.

SUSAN

I'm not so sure that's true, the evidence would suggest otherwise… but either way that's what it's going to take, a lot of hard work, to put this right.

PASTOR

I want to put things right.

SUSAN

(Chuckles) That would make a great national moto… do you know any jokes, any real jokes, like knock, knock, who's there?

PASTOR

Not really no I'm sorry to say, I never… well perhaps one. I heard it many years ago at a conference. Who was the only prophet in the bible to have cosmetic surgery?… Eyes-Higher.

SUSAN

Yeah… *(They embrace)*   How does Mum put up with you?

PASTOR

She has a much better sense of humour.

SUSAN

Now that's more like it. Still… needs work though, an awful lot of work.

LIGHTS OUT – LIGHTS RISE ON TRASH ISLAND – The reggae version of the hymn. Is heard. Bal and Nazreen – voices only -

Eternal Father, strong to save,
Whose arm hath bound the restless wave,
Who bidd'st the mighty ocean deep
Its own appointed limits keep;
Oh, hear us when we cry to Thee,
For those in peril on the sea!

The sound of the sea and gulls – LIGHTS OUT.

END

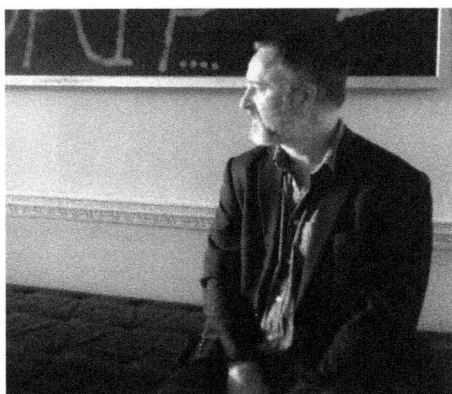

Neil S. Reddy photo by Sue Hall

www.ingramcontent.com/pod-product-compliance
Lightning Source LLC
Chambersburg PA
CBHW032112040426
42337CB00040B/238